AFTER DEATH THEN WHAT?

ARE YOU READY TO DIE?

WESLEY SMITH

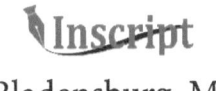

Bladensburg, MD

Published by Inscript Books
a division of Dove Christian Publishers
P.O. Box 611
Bladensburg, MD 20710-0611
www.inscriptpublishing.com

Scriptures taken from the King James Version of the Holy Bible, public domain

Quotations marked ESV are taken from The ESV® Bible (The Holy Bible, English Standard Version®) copyright © 2001 by Crossway, a publishing ministry of Good News Publishers.

Quotations marked NIV are taken from THE HOLY BIBLE, NEW INTERNATIONAL VERSION®, NIV® Copyright © 1973, 1978, 1984, 2011 by Biblical, Inc.® Used by permission. All rights reserved worldwide.

Quotations marked NLT are taken from the Holy Bible, New Living Translation, copyright © 1996, 2004, 2015 by Tyndale House Foundation. Used by permission of Tyndale House Publishers, Inc., Carol Stream, Illinois 60188. All rights reserved.

Inscript and the portrayal of a pen with script are trademarks of Dove Christian Publishers.

Book Design by Mark Yearnings
ISBN: 978-1-7375177-1-9
Copyright © 2021 by Wesley Smith
All Rights Reserved
Printed in the United States of America

Dedications

I dedicate this book to two of my cousins, who have gone on to be with the Lord: Kiyan Yearby, a two-year-old who died from heart failure, and Martha Smith, who died from the Covid-19 virus.

I started this book five years ago, but their back-to-back deaths pushed me to finish this book. Thank You, Kiyan & Martha; may you continue to rest in peace. You will continue to live in our hearts.

I also dedicate this book to my auntie Mary McDowell. My aunt passed just as I was putting the final touches on this book. She was in and out of the hospital for the past few years with health issues. The doctors sent her home to hospice care to be with her beloved family and friends. They sent her home to say goodbye.

Our family has a family prayer line, where we come together by conference call every Saturday morning at 6:00 am to pray. In her last months with us, she would find the strength to get up and lead us in prayer. She would always give us words of encouragement.

She told us that God had spoken to her and told her that He was on His way, so "get your house in order, Mary." She reminded us that she did not know when He was coming, but she had her bags packed and she was ready to go, and none of our prayers would hold her back from being in the presence of God.

I got a chance to travel to visit my auntie a week before transition. She was full of love and high spirit, with excitement. Knowing that her ride to heaven was on the way. She left us with such hope, knowing that the peace of God is real. She was indeed a true soldier to the end. Thank you, Aunt Mary; you will always live with us.

Table of Contents

Dedications .... **iii**

Forewords **1**

Introduction **9**

Chapter 1

What is Death? **13**

Seventeen Different Religions Beliefs of Live After Death 14

Chapter 2

Is the Medical Field Replacing God? **20**

Machine as Master 21
Flexible Rule 22

Chapter 3

My Experiences as a Teacher in the Prison and Jail System **24**

Chapter 4

What the Bible Says About Death **27**

The Nature of Man 27
Does the Soul Die? 28
What Is a Soul? 29
Where Do Christians Go When They Die? 30
Who are the Dead in Christ? 32

Chapter 5

Is There Really a Hell? **34**

Muslims Beliefs on Hell 34
The Jehovah's Witnesses Beliefs on Hell 38
The Seventh-day Adventists Beliefs On Hell 38
Christians Beliefs about Hell 40

Chapter 6

Getting Your House in Order **43**

Preparing for Death ... 45
Things We Need to Get in Order Before Death ... 45

Chapter 7

Burial / Life Insurance / Wills ... **50**

Let's get started… ... 51
Why Is It Called Life Insurance? ... 51
What is Life Insurance? ... 51
Banking / Saving Accounts ... 52
What Is a Will and Why Do I Need One? ... 52

Chapter 8

Passing The Mantle to Your Successor ... **56**

Different Roles ... 57

Chapter 9

Pre-Planning Your Funeral ... **59**

The Biggest Decision You Should Make: Burial, Cremation, or Donation? ... 59

Chapter 10

Coping With the Loss of Your Loved One ... **66**

Coping With the Loss of a Loved One ... 67
How Do I Move on With Life? ... 68
How Psychologists Can Help ... 70
How Christian Based Grief Counseling Helps ... 70
Ways to Cope ... 71
Living a Godly Life ... 71
Moving On ... 72
Stories Of Those Who Have Lost Loved Ones ... 72

Final Words ... **85**

Endnotes ... **87**

Forewords

Honored to give a foreword gesture to Servant Wesley Smith's new book, *After Death, Then What?* I've known Wesley since high school, where we competed on the basketball court. He was a fierce defensive competitor who got thrilled guarding the best player on the opposite team. Outside the court, he was also known for being intelligent and fierce, but in the wrong direction. His savvy and street reputation preceded him.

The enemy had determined that Wesley was going to die—SOON. But just as GOD gave Hezekiah time to live once he turned his head toward the wall and prayed, GOD gave the same grace and mercy to Wesley Smith, not only to live but to forever GIVE. This powerful lion has evolved from the jungle to give us a breathtaking subject we usually run away from: *After Death.*

The book gives us a brief global journey on how famous religions view after death. He peeks into their values, beliefs, and doctrines to allow you to fairly evaluate what you may or may not believe. Most books give their readers their hypothesis and literature but rarely give us different perspectives and views. *After Death, Then What* looks death in the face and says, "Think for yourself."

After this book glimpses at the content of other major religions, Servant Wesley boldly places their content about After death at the door of Christianity. The Word naturally explains itself, but Servant gives us a down-home interpretation with research and intelligence. He gets input from young adults who are lost but need help. With his own life experience near death, he eloquently gives water to the thirsty, food to those who are hungry, and resuscitation to all of us who need to be revitalized. While we are encouraged to look and discuss after death, this book also allows us to talk about pre-planning before death. How often do families fall out and/or are put in financial jams because no one was prepared? *After Death, Then What* allows us to moonwalk before death by equipping us to talk before we walk—to the grave.

As we all ponder our lives amid a deadly pandemic(s), this book gives us a spiritual shot in the arm while leading us to evaluate our existence now and the life after death.

Humbly,
Min. Guy Wheeler, MSW, MCAP, CCJAP

***

This book will be a great read for all. As I began to read the book, I thought to myself *a book about death*. Is this something I want to read? To my delight, the book was amazing. It tackled some of the very things that we do not want to deal with. After much time and several chapters later, I realized as a husband, pastor, and father how this book could be used to enlighten individuals on this very touchy but necessary subject. The author did a tremendous job outlining and arranging the book so that all readers are able to understand the need to have their things in order. From a biblical and secular standpoint, we all need this book. I want to thank the author for his obedience in the writing of this book and for sharing his personal experiences throughout the book.

Grateful,
Pastor Christopher Woods
Pursuit Worship Center
West Park, Florida

***

In the beginning, God created heaven and earth. A paradise for all of his creations made in his image: man, woman, their offspring, and animals (Genesis 1:27). In this beautiful garden was peace, love, harmony, and long life. Today, we are living in disharmonious times, where humans feel so disconnected from God's paradise and original plan that rather than embrace life, they question the purpose of death.

After Death, Then What? Are you Ready to Die? This question posed by Pastor/Servant Wesley Smith is both universal and profound. In his book, Servant Wesley answers these questions for any man or woman, teen, or child. More importantly, he assists us in understanding how humans left God's paradise for self-imprisonment.

Understanding that the Bible is the only book that God gave to be saved by Jesus Christ and frees man from this incarcerated state, Servant Wesley gives a complete origin of man's creation from the dust of the earth by God by leading the reader through the first book of the Bible, Genesis, and subsequently to the book of Revelation, the last book in the Bible.

The arrangement of the book *After Death, Then What?* follows the Biblical narrative which tells the beginning of mankind and highlights the decisions that lead to man's broken relationship with God. Ironically, the first decision can be traced back to a question posed by the serpent to Eve, the mother of all of the living. Servant Wesley's understanding of the meaning and results of the serpent's questions, "Hath God Said," which causes Eve to lie and encourage Adam to eat the forbidden fruit, sets the stage for understanding how humans lose their fellowship with God. This disobedience resulted in a spiritual death and ultimately a fear of a physical death.

Notably, as man strives to seek to understand the sorrows associated with death, they turn to the book of Psalms, which has more teardrops than any other book in the Bible. More importantly, Servant Wesley inspires the reader to deepen their understanding of life and assess their misunderstanding about death. Congratulations to Servant Wesley Smith for his book, *After Death, Then What? Are you Ready to Die?*, a well-thought-out spiritual guide that assists men, women, and children with their reconnection to God. May God continue to bless you and your readers.

Sincerely Yours in Christ,
Reverend Harvey N. Quarles
Father-in-Law and Brother in Christ
Philadelphia, Pennsylvania

***

Someone once remarked that "death is not the opposite of life, but a part of it." None of us can deny that death is an ever-present reality that we face. In human existence, we are born, we live, and eventually, we die. Along with the celebration of births that occur daily, there is mourning over the loss of life with the same regularity. World Health Organization data estimates that over 55 million people die each year. Statistics from the U.S. government reveal that more than 3 million people died in America in 2020. That figure was an increase of 12% from 2019 data, undoubtedly due to the global pandemic. Nonetheless, millions of people each year are being claimed by death. The knowledge that death is unavoidable and inescapable should motivate us to prepare for its eventuality in our lives and families. Though it is unpleasant to consider, and we are reluctant to think about it while enjoying life, the impact that death will make demands that we consider how we will face it when it comes. To that end, Servant Wesley Smith has thoughtfully and systematically presented a guide to help us navigate the process of understanding, preparing for, and coping with death. Utilizing research, keen insight, and personal anecdotes, he leads us to a place where death is not feared but accepted and not ignored but planned for. Along with helping one prepare for death, this book points the reader to the reality of the afterlife. Various religious views are presented, but the theological position of Christianity is upheld and encouraged. Through this worldview, God graciously gives us life to live as we choose, but our choices and behavior while here will determine where we spend eternity.

Everyone who reads this book will be benefitted. The fearful and uninformed will be educated, believers will be validated, unbelievers will be challenged, and all will be comforted if they follow the advice offered. *After Death, Then What?* will take the mystery out of death and answer the question that it poses.

Bishop Patrick L. Kelly
Pastor, Cathedral Church of God
Pompano Beach, Florida

***

To my spiritual son and daughter, Pastor Wesley, and sister Rosalind.

I find this book to be a true breathing version of Matthew 6:10; "God's Kingdom come, God's will be done on earth as it is in heaven." May you continue to cry loud and spare not.

I wish I could have had this wisdom, knowledge, and understanding 45 years ago. The book of Ecclesiastes 3:1-2; "to everything there is a time and season, and a time to every purpose under the son. A time to be born and a time to die." As the old song says, "Get right church and let's go home."

Pastor Alfred Taylor
Winter Haven, Florida

***

What a blessing and honor to be asked to do the foreword to this book. We have known Wesley, Rosalind, his beautiful wife and partner in ministry, and his family for many years. We met him shortly after he was released from prison. He went away to a treatment program and returned with the love of his life, Rosalind. God gave them to us as our son and daughter to mentor, disciple, and release them to fulfill the awesome call on their lives. They have and shall continue to be a threat to the kingdom of darkness. We are honored and humbled by God's choosing us to partner with Him to be a part of His plan for Wesley and Rosalind's life.

This book is compelling and to the point. The title, "After Death, Then What? It shows Pastor Wesley's hard work and honesty as to how he faces the reality of death and how he wants his readers to have that same realistic view.

This book is a must-read. You will find out the beliefs about death of the medical field, religious groups, and what the Bible has to say. His focused research shows us that we can be more informed facing the inevitable reality of death. He contends that death is a certainty of life. Read this book with an open mind, and you will be amazed at the wealth of both spiritual and practical knowledge you will gain.

Pastor Wesley takes us through all the facets of the issue of death, from preplanning, life insurance/wills, funeral planning, to how to deal with the grief that follows. This book is packed with scriptural references to support God's point of view on the matters of life and death.

Praise God! This is a book to be shared with others.

Elders Arthur and Patricia Holsey

Introduction

After writing my first book, "Grace and Mercy," by the inspiration of God, many people would ask me, "When are you writing your next book?" I would push them away by saying that I was waiting on the Lord when the Lord had already given me two topics to write about. One was "The Extended Parents," which we call stepfamilies, and the second was " After Death-Then What?" Are You Ready to Die?" These are two topics that are very personal to me.

First, I was introduced to one of my two sisters at the early age of 7. My father told me that she was my stepsister. I was truly confused; who stepped on her? She was as loving and beautiful as my other sister; I saw no difference. I knew as a kid that this was a bad label to put on a family member, and I knew that one day I would have to make a difference.

Second, "After Death, Then What? Are you Ready to Die?" Of course, no one is truly ready to die, but the truth of the matter is that we will all die one day.

Hebrews 9:27; "And it is appointed unto men

once to die, but after this the judgment."

In my 64 years here on earth, I've seen many people be born, and I've seen many people die. Many people have mixed feelings about what happens after death. Do we really die? Why would God allow good people to die so young? etc.

I lost a grandson (Jay), who was at the early age of two when he passed. This really put a challenge on my faith. I was so angry with God. How, Lord, can you allow such a young, innocent soul to die so young? My daughter (Jay's mother) told me, "Dad, you are going to do the eulogy." I did not want to do this, but I could not let her down at a time like this. I now had to face and trust the God that I was angry with. He met me where I was and enabled me to carry this service through...He did it again.

It would be one thing if these were feelings of others, but they were also my own feelings. After accepting Jesus into my life, many of my questions were answered. But what about all those who have not come to a true godly understanding of death? I've witnessed many of my brothers and sisters in Christ really lose it when they lose a loved one. <u>Their faith and belief in Christ are tested, and now they are without hope. As saints, we say that we are believers, but there comes a time when we are tested to see if we truly believe.</u> Many people are afraid to even have a family discussion about death. Realizing the season that we are living in, people are dying at a rate as never before.

I felt inspired that *"After Death, Then What? Are you Ready to Die?"* should be my next book.

My prayer is that you are inspired to have a clearer godly consciousness of the truth of death as God, the creator of life and death, sees it.

As a pastor, I had the opportunity to counsel many families as they prepared to funeralize their loved ones. Many did not have a clue of what to do nor how to plan for the services. I now see death as a time to celebrate the life of the one that has gone to the other side. I would like to share with you a few of my experiences.

> *Ecclesiastes 7:1-4 (NIV): A good reputation is more valuable than the most expensive perfume. The day one dies is better than the day he is born!* **2** *It is better to spend your time at funerals than at festivals. For you are going to die, and it is a good thing to think about it while there is still time.* **3** *Sorrow is better than laughter, for sadness has a refining influence on us.* **4** *Yes, a wise man thinks much of death, while the fool thinks only of having a good time now.*

Experience #1: I was called by a family to come and mediate between their differences. Their brother was about to go to the other side (he was on life support); he was married for two years. The wife said that he did not want to live on life support, and she wanted to pull the plug to honor his wishes. The family said that she just wanted him to die so that she could collect the insurance money.

As I sat and listened to them go back and forth, I was asking the Lord, "What will you have me to do?" He said, "Let's pray." As we held hands and prayed, we were inviting God into our meeting. This brought all of us to realize that God will have to be the one to comfort us and give us some direction. And He did (they were a Christian family). As I prepared to leave, they all thanked me for allowing God to use me. I never knew what they came to agree on, but when I left, they were all on one accord.

When I got into my car, I realized that this was not all about them; this was about me and my family. My wife and I have written wills already. I, too, have a strong family. I do not want to leave my wife in this situation. I believe that when we lose a loved one, we need this time to grieve and mourn. So, I made an amendment to our will. "If I ever need to be put on life support to live, let me stay on it for seven days, and on the eighth day (new beginning), pull the plug; if someone does not agree, tell them to come see me." This is why we need to be "Prepared to Die"; we need to have our houses in order.

Chapter 1
What is Death?

Although intellectually, we all know that one day we shall die, generally, we are so reluctant to think of our death that this knowledge does not touch our hearts, and we live our lives as if we are going to be in this world forever. As a result, the things of this world, such as material possessions, reputation, popularity, and the pleasures of the senses, become of paramount importance. So, we devote almost all our time and energy to obtaining them and engage in many negative actions for their sake. We are so preoccupied with the concerns of this life that there is little room in our minds for genuine spiritual practice. When the time of death actually arrives, we discover that by having ignored death all our lives, we are completely unprepared.[1]

When the body disintegrates at death the soul and spirit does not cease.

Death is the separation of the connection between our body and soul/spirit. Most people believe that death takes place when the heart stops beating. Death occurs when the subtle consciousness finally leaves the body to go to the next life. The body is like a guesthouse; the soul and spirit is a guest; when we die, our soul and spirit has to leave this body and enter into another body, like a guest leaving one guesthouse and traveling to another.[2]

"Are You Ready to Die?"

I would like to take you on a tour with me as we travel into the mindset and beliefs of others and hear their personal testimonies, doctrines, culture, and religious beliefs of what death means to them. Then we will sit at the foot of Jesus and see what He has to say about it. I will prepare the table for you and allow you to choose what you will partake of. But remember, your conscious is yours to live and die with. I've come to the conclusion that death is only a part of life. It is the vehicle that takes one from time into eternity. The question is, where will death take you?

Seventeen Different Religions Beliefs of Live After Death

My research was obtained from their bibles (books of guidance) and one-on-one conversations with believers of different religions. I will also give you scriptures referencing my findings. I will share my findings with you below.

New Age

Human reincarnations occur until a person reaches oneness with God. No eternal life as a resurrection person. No literal heaven or hell.

Judaism

There will be a physical resurrection. The obedient will live forever with God, and the unrighteous will suffer. Some Jews do not believe in a conscious life after death.

Hinduism

Reincarnation into a better status (good karma) if a person has behaved well. If one has been bad, he can be reborn and pay for past sins (bad karma) by suffering.

Hare Krishna

Those who are unenlightened continue in endless reincarnation (rebirth on earth) based on the sinful acts of a person's previous life.

Transcendental Meditation

Reincarnation based on karma (reaping the consequences of one's actions) until loss of sell into union with Brahman. No heaven or hell.

Buddhists

People do not have a soul or spirit. However, one's desires and fallings may be reincarnated into another's person. No heaven or hell.

Nichiren Shōshū Buddhism

Repeated reincarnation until one is awakened to the Buddha nature. then reincarnation ends. No heaven or hell.

Islam

Resurrection of bodies. Final day of reckoning

and rewards. Eternal paradise for those who believe in Islam. Eternal hell for infidels, those who reject Islam.

Baha'i World Faith

Personal immortality based on good works, with rewards for the faithful. Heaven and hell are conditions, not places.

Mormonism (Latter-day Saints)

Eventually nearly everyone goes to one of three separate heavenly 'kingdoms", with some achieving godhood. Apostates and murderers go to "outer darkness.

Jehovah's witnesses (Watchtower Bible & Tract Society)

The 144,000 live as spirits in heaven. The rest of the righteous, "the great crowd," live on earth, and must obey God perfectly for 1000 years or be annihilated.

Armstrongism

Resurrected believers will live on the new earth. Unsaved will face judgment.

Unification Church

After death one goes to the spirit world. There is no resurrection. Members advance by convincing others to follow Sun Myung Moon. Everyone will be saved, even Satan

Christian Science

Death is not real. Heaven and hell are states of mind. The way to reach heaven is by attaining harmony (oneness with God).

Unity School of Christianity

Death is a result of wrong thinking. One moves to a different body (reincarnation) until enlightenment. No literal heaven or hell.

Spiritualism (Spiritism)

After life on this earthly plane, life continues in the spirit world, where one's spirit may progress from one level to another. Heaven and hell are states of mind. Some believe in reincarnation.

Scientology

Hell is a myth. People who get clear of engrams become operating thetans.

Hebrew Israelite Beliefs

Hebrew Israelites believe both heaven and hell are conditions – mere "states of mind."

***

Above are the beliefs of 18 major religions. This information was gathered from the book, "Christianity, Cults & Religion."[1]

If I have erred on any of the above information, I apologize. My research was obtained from their bibles (books of guidance) and one-on-one conversations with believers of their different religions.

Now comes the question: *What do you believe?*

---

1 Christianity, Cults & Religion, Paul Carden, Rose Publishing

What foundation supports your belief?

Christianity

I Thessalonians 4:13-17 *(ESV): But we do not want you to be uninformed, brothers and sisters, about those who are asleep (death), that you may be not grieved as others do who have no hope. For since we believe that Jesus died and rose again, even so, through Jesus, God will bring with Him those who have fallen asleep (death). For this we declare to you by a word from the Lord, will not proceed those who have fallen asleep (death). For the Lord himself will descend from heaven with a cry of command, with the voice of an archangel, and with the sound of the trumpet of God. And the dead in Christ will rise first. Then we who are alive, who are left, will be caught up together with them in the clouds to meet the Lord in the air, and so we will always be with the Lord...*

1 Corinthians 15:50-58 *(NLT):* [50] *What I am saying, dear brothers and sisters, is that our physical bodies cannot inherit the Kingdom of God. These dying bodies cannot inherit what will last forever.* [51] *But let me reveal to you a wonderful secret. We will not all die, but we will all be transformed!*

[52] *It will happen in a moment, in the blink of an eye, when the last trumpet is blown. For when the trumpet sounds, those who have died will be raised to live forever. And we who are living will also be*

transformed. ⁵³ *For our dying bodies must be transformed into bodies that will never die; our mortal bodies must be transformed into immortal bodies.* ⁵⁴ *Then, when our dying bodies have been transformed into bodies that will never die,[a] this Scripture will be fulfilled: "Death is swallowed up in victory.[b]* ⁵⁵ *O death, where is your victory? O death, where is your sting?[c]"* ⁵⁶ *For sin is the sting that results in death, and the law gives sin its power.* ⁵⁷ *But thank God! He gives us victory over sin and death through our Lord Jesus Christ.* ⁵⁸ *So, my dear brothers and sisters, be strong and immovable. Always work enthusiastically for the Lord, for you know that nothing you do for the Lord is ever useless.*

Chapter 2

Is the Medical Field Replacing God?

Death had always seemed a relatively simple and clearly definable end to life. It came when a man stopped breathing, and his heart stopped beating. Today, that definition needs an added definition. With mechanical heart and breathing aids, and intravenous feedings, doctors can keep patients technically alive in hospitals for months or even years while they are in a deep coma.

Many physicians now believe that the question "Is this patient dead?" should be answered largely on the basis of his electroencephalogram (EEC or "brain wave") tracings.

"Although the heart has been enthroned through the ages as the sacred chalice of life's blood," says Boston's Neurosurgeon Dr. Hannibal Hamlin, "the human spirit is the product of man's brain, not his heart." Yet generally, in legal practice, a pronouncement of death is based only upon the heart having stopped beating and takes no account of the brain.

Machine as Master

To decide just when the human spirit is gone, just when the intricate machinery should be turned off and the heart allowed to stop, is far more than a legal problem. It involves the doctor as deeply as it does the patient or his anguished kin. Trained from his first day in medical school that his duty is to save and prolong life, the physician may not only resort to extraordinary measures, but he may continue them even after a flat EEG line (meaning no electrical activity in the brain) has persisted so long that there can be no real hope of recovery.

When the physician decides to support the patient with mechanical aids after the EEG has gone flat, says Surgeon Charles F. Zukoski III of the VA Hospital in Nashville, he runs the risk of letting the *machine become his master.* Slowly but inexorably, the blood pressure will fall until it can no longer support the kidneys or other vital organs. "This," says Dr. Zukoski, "is an agonal type of death. We can carry the prolongation of so-called life too far."

All that mechanical aids can do after the brain has reached its point of no return, says Dr. Hamlin, is to "maintain the look of life in the face of death." And at a frightful cost in both money and emotion. The patient's family, says Harvard's Dr. Robert S. Schwab, suffers cruelly and may have to pay $250 a day for apparatus which is merely sending blood through an organism that is otherwise dead. "When," he asks, "do you pull the plug out and make this expensive equipment available to someone who might live?"

Flexible Rule

At Massachusetts General Hospital, the criterion laid down by Neurologist Schwab is that the EEG must remain flat for about 24 hours and stay flat despite external stimuli such as a loud noise.

There must be no muscular or pupillary reflexes; the patient must have no heartbeat or respiration of his own—only what the machines are providing. "After that," says Dr. Schwab, "the physician in charge can agree to turn off the artificial aids and pronounce the patient dead."

How long the EEG must remain flat depends on circumstances. After barbiturate poisoning or long exposure to extreme cold, a patient might have a flat EEG for several hours and still be capable of full recovery. Dr. Schwab would leave the precise timing to the physician's judgment in each case.

The question of when to "pull the plug" and let death occur has acquired new urgency with the practice of transplanting kidneys and other vital organs. Transplant surgeons want organs as fresh as possible; the chance that a cadaver kidney will work well in the recipient patient is vastly increased if it can be removed immediately after circulation has stopped. But in the U.S., as in most countries, it would be illegal to remove a kidney from a patient who has not yet been pronounced dead.

Sweden's Dr. Clarence Crafoord, one of the world's greatest heart-lung surgeons, caused a public outcry earlier when he suggested that a person should be declared dead when a flat EEG pattern shows that his brain has definitely and irrevocably ceased to function. Dr. Crafoord was concerned about truly hopeless cases, but the kin of patients being kept alive with mechanical aids jumped to the conclusion that he meant the devices should be shut off, the patients declared dead, and their organs used for transplants.

This led to worried talk about "cannibalizing" human beings, like airplanes or autos, to get usable spare parts for others. France's National Academy of Medicine added to the furor by proposing that a patient may be adjudged dead if the EEG has shown no brain activity for 48 hours.

After that, the academy recommended, surgeons should be allowed to remove vital organs for transplantation even before the artificial circulation is shut off.

No country is yet ready to give such proposals legal sanction. But there is no doubt that modern medical technology leaves present laws, as well as physicians' traditional precepts and practices, out of date on essential matters of life and death.[3]

Chapter 3

My Experiences as a Teacher in the Prison and Jail System

I have been an active volunteer worker in jails and prisons for over 30 years. I teach life skills classes for the youth and adult men. I once had one of my adult male classes write out their eulogy as a class assignment. There were about forty men in this class. Only three did the assignment. The others told me that they didn't want to talk about death. Wow...most of these men were gang bangers, hustlers from the violent streets, men who saw death weekly. Yet, they feared talking about death.

I, too, grew up fearing death. No one taught me that death was a part of life. We were told things like, "stay out of the graveyard." I never understood why we could not play in the graveyard; dead people could not do us any harm. It was the living that we should be afraid of.

Today I understand that death is a significant and inevitable part of life. As I began to talk about it, sharing to others how I feel and what I think about it, I began to understand God's plan for life, and that death is a part of His plan. It began to take the edge of fear away from me and to give me peace about it. Yes,, it's still a challenge to think of losing a loved one. So, today I choose to focus more on what I do have. I have life today, and I plan to use this time wisely, spending time with the ones I love, not allowing our disagreements to divide us for any long period of time. Tomorrow is not promised to any of us.

I will not leave the pressure on my loved ones to make decisions or how to prepare for my funeral services. I will set my house in order while I am still in this earthly house. I have already made out my will. I encourage you to also. I must admit it was not easy for me to visit my own funeral. As I faced that giant, I was then able to overcome the fear of death.

Hosea 4:6 "My people are destroyed for lack of knowledge: because thou hast rejected knowledge" of God, that is lack of piety (reverence for God); their ignorance was willful, as the epithet (a descriptive phrase expressing a quality characteristic of the person or thing mentioned). The phrase my people implies they ought to have known, having the opportunity, as the people of God.

I interviewed ten youth, ages 15-17, who were incarcerated. These youth were facing long sentences for very violent crimes. With the life that they were living, they faced death every single day. They had very little to say about death. Most of them had seen many of their friends killed by acts of violence.

One of the questions I asked the young men was, "How would you define death?" Here are their answers:

1. Devonte-17; someone going to sleep and never waking up.
2. Gavin-17; when life is over / life is suffering.
3. Steven-17; reactions of your parents going crazy
4. Dave-16; when the heart stops breathing
5. Jiovnni-17; no love, no thinking, no feelings
6. Jatvos-16; a dream in which we have no control
7. Louis-16; end of life on earth
8. Tavaren-15; tragedy
9. Dylan-17; end of your purpose on earth
10. Javan-16; eye-opener

As we can see, we all have our own views, beliefs, and fears about death. You would not take your car to a carpenter to repair it for you. No, you would take it back to the one that has knowledge of the original blueprints of that car. I choose to believe in the one that created me (God).

So let's take a closer look at what the Bible has to say about life, death, and the afterlife.

Chapter 4

What the Bible Says About Death

What really happens to a person when they die? Is there really heaven and hell? The answer to these questions may surprise many of you. You are about to find out that what you believe may not line up with what the Bible says about death. The Bible is very clear about the state of death. I pray that you have an open mind as you read the information I've studied from the Bible.

The Nature of Man

We must first establish the facts about the nature of man. The first Bible text we need to look at is Job 4:17: "Can a mortal be more righteous than God? Can even a strong man be more pure than his Maker?" The word mortal means subject to death; the word immortal means not subject to death.

The word immortal is used only once in the Bible, 1 Timothy 1:17: "*Now unto the King eternal (immortal), invisible, the only wise God, be honor and glory forever, amen."* God is the only One who has immortality. 1 Timothy 6:16: *"who alone can never die [immortal], who lives in light so terrible that no human being can approach him. No mere man has ever seen him nor ever will. Unto him be honor and everlasting power and dominion forever and ever. Amen."* Only God has this power of immortal existence. Man is described as being mortal or subject to death.

Does the Soul Die?

Some people believe that the body and the soul are immortal and that the soul itself cannot die. This is why I am not leaning to my own understanding about death; I am leaning on the Word of God and the Word of God alone. Ezekiel 18:4: *"Behold, all souls are mine; as the soul of the father, so also the soul of the son is mine: the soul that sinneth,* **it shall die.***"*

The text says that the soul is subject to death. I found no doctrine in the Bible that says that the soul is immortal.

Since the text states that the soul is subject to death, then where did this belief originate that the soul does not die? When studying the Bible, we must first go to Genesis (which means beginning) to find where things originated. We can look at the beginning of the Bible and find out who is responsible for this lie.

We can read Genesis 3:1-4:

"The serpent was the craftiest of all the

creatures the Lord God had made. So the serpent came to the woman. 'Really?' he asked. 'None of the fruit in the garden? God says you mustn't eat any of it?' 'Of course we may eat it,' the woman told him.

'It's only the fruit from the tree at the center of the garden that we are not to eat. God says we mustn't eat it or even touch it, **or we will die.'**[4] *'That's a lie!' the serpent hissed.* **You'll not die!'"**

The conversation is between the Serpent and Eve. In vs. 4, the serpent said that "you'll not die." Here at the very beginning of mankind, Satan originated the very first lie that the soul would not die, and this lie has been carried down through the ages.

What Is a Soul?

Ecclesiastes 12:6-8; [6] *Yes, remember your Creator now while you are young— before the silver cord of life snaps and the gold bowl is broken; before the pitcher is broken at the fountain and the wheel is broken at the cistern;* [7]**then the dust returns to the earth as it was, and the spirit returns to God who gave it.** [8]*All is futile, says the Preacher; utterly futile.*

Verse 7 states that the spirit shall return unto God who gave it. What does it mean when it speaks of the spirit?

Job 27:3; [3] *All the while my breath is in me, and the spirit of God is in my nostrils.*

This text shows us that the spirit, which God gives to man, is in his nostrils.

> *Genesis 2:7; "And the Lord God formed man of the dust of the ground, and breathed into his nostrils the breath of life; and man became a living soul."*

God breathed into man's nostrils at creation, and that breath of life is the spirit that returns to God.

The words *breath* and *spirit* are used interchangeably in the Bible, meaning the life which God gave man. The breath and/or spirit is how man lives. The body of mankind was formed out of the dust of the ground, and then God breathed life into man, and he became a living soul.[4]

> *Psalms 104:29-30;* [29]*Thou hidest thy face, they are troubled: thou takest away their breath, they die, and return to their dust.*[30] *Thou sendest forth thy spirit, they are created: and thou renewest the face of the earth.*

Life and death are described together, and the words breath and spirit are used the same. Also, remember when studying the Bible, when we see *spirit* in lower case, it refers to the human spirit. When it is in upper case, it is speaking of the Holy Spirit.

Where Do Christians Go When They Die?[5]

John said in Revelation 21:2:

"I saw the Holy City, New Jerusalem,

coming down out of heaven from God."

The New Jerusalem that Jesus is preparing for us will descend out of the current Heaven and reside on a recreated Earth. That is our ultimate destination as believers. But the moment Christians die, we immediately depart from this world into the presence of God. How do I know that?

Look at what the Scripture says about the immediacy (quality of bringing one into direct and instant involvement) of our entrance into God's presence. A Christian goes immediately into the presence of God.

In Luke 23:43, Jesus said to the thief on the cross who had just exercised faith:

"Today you shall be with Me in Paradise."

Acts 7:59 says:

"Stephen...called on the Lord and said, 'Lord Jesus, receive my spirit!"

But the seminal passage in the Bible that describes what happens to Christians when they die is 2 Corinthians 5:1:

"For we know that if our earthly house of this tabernacle were dissolved, we have a building of God, a house not made with hands, eternal in the heavens...."

Paul said our bodies are like a tent. Who wants to live in a tent for eternity? Our bodies are a temporary dwelling, a tent that will be put away one day.

In 2 Corinthians 5:6, Paul says:

> *"While we are at home in the body,*
> *we are absent from the Lord."*

We cannot be in two locations at once. As long as we are here, we cannot also be in Heaven with God. That is what Paul was saying. We think this world is our home, but it is not. It is a temporary location. Yes, we have people we love here. Yes, God has given us an assignment here. But it is temporary. As long as we are here, we are not at home with the Lord.

Paul went on to say in 2 Corinthians 5:8:

> *"We are of good courage, I say, and*
> *prefer rather to be absent from the body*
> *and to be at home with the Lord."*

He was saying, "I prefer to be once for all absent from the body so that I can be once for all at home with the Lord."

That is what happens to Christians when we die. The moment we leave this body, we are forever at home with the Lord.

When we die, our spirit goes to be with the Lord awaiting the final resurrection body we will receive at the Rapture.

In 1 Thessalonians 4:16, Paul said:

> *"The Lord Himself will descend from*
> *heaven with a shout, with the voice of the*
> *archangel and with the trumpet of God,*
> *and the dead in Christ will rise first."*

Who are the Dead in Christ?[6]

They are Christians who have already died. Their spirits are in Heaven, their bodies are in the ground, but at the Rapture, their bodies will be raised, and then that generation of believers who are alive at that time will also be caught up, and together they will meet the Lord in the air.

The Lord will descend, you and I who are in Heaven with God will descend, and 1 Corinthians 15:52 says at that moment:

*"...in the twinkling of an eye...the
dead will be raised imperishable,
and we will be changed."*

Read 1 Corinthians chapter 15 (mortal and immortality).

At the Rapture, we will receive a brand-new body that is forever free from suffering and death. *(The word "Rapture" is not in the bible, it is a translation from the Greek equivalent "harpazo," which means to seize, snatch, or carry away).*

Chapter 5

Is There Really a Hell?

Many people today have many different views about hell or if there is really a hell at all. Some say that they are living in hell right here on earth. I was led to do my own studies and research to see what different religions believe about hell. My research was obtained from their bibles (books of guidance) and one on one conversations with believers of their different religions. I will also give you scriptures referencing my findings. I will share my findings with you below.

Muslims Beliefs on Hell[7]

Yes, Muslims do believe in hell just the way Christians do, except that their concept of hell is a little bit different from that of Christians in the sense that they believe that for some sinners, hell isn't a permanent place of suffering as many Christians see it. According to Muslims, the punishment that certain sinners receive in hell is temporary in the sense that these sinners don't stay in hell forever. Certain sinners will be set free from hell and brought to paradise after paying for the sins they committed while on Earth.

The Day of Judgment (the Last Day)[8]

When a person dies, they remain in the grave and wait to be resurrected on the Last Day. While waiting in their graves, deceased souls bound for hell (Jahannam) experience some suffering (although they are not yet in hell) in the sense that they do not have peace. But deceased souls bound for paradise (Jannah) experience peace while they wait in their graves to be resurrected and taken to paradise.

According to Islam, on the Last Day (that is the Earth's final day), the whole world will be destroyed by Allah, and he will raise all dead people, including jinn (supernatural creatures), in order to judge them according to their deeds. During the judging process, Allah will decide whether a person will go to paradise (Jannah) or hell (Jahannam). Only Allah has the power to judge and decide who goes to hell and who goes to paradise.

Islam's names for Hell[9]

There are so many names that hell is called in Islam. The most common name for hell in Islam is Jahannam.

Every Muslim knows that Jahannam means hell. Other names for hell include *The Fire, Blazing Fire, The Abyss, The Blaze,* and *That which Breaks to Pieces.*

Facts About Hell in Islam[10]

- According to Islam, hell is so deep that if one were to drop a stone into it, it would take 70 years for the stone to hit the bot-

tom of hell.
- Suffering in hell is both physical and spiritual.
- Not every sinner waits until the Last Day to be judged by Allah and sent to hell. Anybody who becomes an "Enemy of Islam" is sent to hell the moment he or she dies. Other groups of sinners, such as those who did not believe in Allah and His Laws and those who died in their sins, will have to wait until the Last Day before entering hell.
- Everybody doesn't suffer the same in hell. The gravity of one's sin will depend on the severity of one's suffering in hell. This means if Mr. A and Mr. B find themselves in hell because they sinned while on Earth, and Mr. A's sins are more severe than that of Mr. B, then Mr. A suffers more in hell than Mr. B. It is as simple as that.
- According to the Quran, hell has seven levels and seven gates. Each gate deals with a specific group or category of sinners. So if the degree of Mr. A's sin is not the same as that of Mr. B's, then they are both going to find themselves at different gates of hell. (Ouran 15:43-44)
- The seven levels of hell contain different forms of torment and torture. The lowest of the levels is considered the severest of all the levels in terms of punishment. This, therefore, means that sinners that find themselves there are considered the worst kinds of sinners.
- Hell is a place where sinners undergo se-

vere forms of torture with things such as fire, boiling water, and scorching wind, which severely scorch sinners' skins to the point where their skins will get destroyed and be replaced with new skins in order for the sinners to start facing their torments afresh. This cycle of torture will carry on for as long as the sinners remain in hell.

- No matter how much a sinner being tortured in hell becomes remorseful and begs for forgiveness, he or she shan't be forgiven.
- No sinner can escape from hell once he or she gets there. The only time a sinner can leave the extreme torture of hell is when he or she has finished paying for his or her transgressions. If a sinner tries to escape from the blazing fire of hell, a hook made of iron will be used to drag the sinner back to hell.
- According to the Quran, hell has nineteen angels who are led by the keeper of hell named Maalik. The Quran describes Maalik as a very severe and harsh man who doesn't feel the plights of the sinners undergoing severe torments. And whenever the inhabitants of hell beg him to let them out of hell, he tells them that they shall remain in hell because they "abhorred the truth" when it was brought to them.
- On top of the blazing fire that exists in hell, the place is also believed to contain a lot of venomous snakes and scorpions. The pain from the venom of any of these snakes and scorpions can last for several decades.

Who Will Go to Hell in Islam[11]

- According to the Quran, the following people shall all end up in hell:
- Disbelievers – these are those who don't believe in Allah
- Polytheists – these are people who believe in more than one god.
- All people who reject the truth
- People who persecute believers
- All sinners and criminals
- Murderers
- The unjust
- People who hide Allah's revelations
- People who commit suicide
- All tyrants
- Hypocrites

The Jehovah's Witnesses Beliefs on Hell

Jehovah's Witnesses believe hell is not a place of eternal suffering but is rather the common grave of humankind. The wicked are annihilated—snuffed out of conscious existence forever.[12]

The Seventh-day Adventists Beliefs On Hell[13]

Silver Spring, Maryland, USA ... [ANN] The Seventh-day Adventist view of hell as annihilation rather than eternal torment is quoted in an October 5 Associated Press (AP) report.

"The Seventh-day Adventist Church, founded in 1863, is best-known for worshiping on Saturday, but annihilationism is another of its distinctive tenets," says Richard N. Ostling, AP religion writer, defining annihilationism as "the unsaved will be lost eternally, but instead of suffering they will simply cease to exist."

Referencing an article in Christianity Today (CT) of the same date, Ostling says that "for conservative Protestants, hell remains a "'burning' issue," with polls indicating "increasing numbers of people [who] no longer believe in the place."

The CT article by Stanley Grenz, a theology professor teaching in British Columbia and Illinois, seeks to answer the question, "Is Hell Forever?"

Identifying annihilationism as a position held by "the 1660 Confession of the General Baptists, the Seventh-day Adventists and several other evangelical groups in the nineteenth century," Grenz says that those who believe this version of "Hell" argue for a better "picture of God."

"They [the annihilationists] argue that because eternal torment serves no remedial purpose, the traditional concept of hell paints a portrait of God as a vindictive despot incompatible with the loving Father in Jesus. Further, they claim that the presence of people in hell throughout eternity contradicts the Christian truth that Christ has conquered every evil foe and God will reconcile all things in Christ," says Grenz.

Grenz does not necessarily accept the annihilationist argument and raises what he calls "substantive problems" in their position. Ostling's conclusion is, "so take your pick: everlasting hell or permanent annihilation. But the Bible's advice would be to do everything possible, spiritually and morally, to escape either fate."

Commenting for the Seventh-day Adventist Church, Angel M. Rodriguez of the Biblical Research Institute says that it's interesting that the issue of "hell" is being raised, even in press reports.

"For the public media to pay attention indicates that this issue is important to people," says Rodriguez."We believe that your convictions about your future destiny is important, and also that God's role and character is critical in this. Eternal torment is not a Biblical view, and cannot be harmonized with a God of love." [Jonathan Gallagher]

Christians Beliefs about Hell[14]

What happens to unbelievers when they die? Just as believers have a current destination (the third Heaven) and a future destination (the New Heaven and Earth), so there is a temporary and eternal destination for the unsaved. The unsaved immediately go to a place called Hades.

Luke 16:23-24 says:

*"In Hades [the rich man] lifted up his
eyes, being in torment, and saw Abraham
far away and Lazarus in his bosom.
And he cried out and said, 'Father
Abraham, have mercy on me, and send
Lazarus so that he may dip the tip of his
finger in water and cool off my tongue,
for I am in agony in this flame.'"*

Hades is the temporary waiting place of the unsaved dead. It is a place of torment that begins

Is There Really a Hell?

the moment an unbeliever dies. That is where the unbelievers go right now, but that is not their final destination.

Their final destination is the Lake of Fire. In Revelation 20:12-15, John said:

> *"I saw the dead, the great and the small, standing before the throne, and books were opened; and another book was opened, which is the book of life; and the dead were judged from the things which were written in the books, according to their deeds. And the sea gave up the dead which were in it, and death and Hades gave up the dead which were in them; and they were judged, every one of them according to their deeds. Then death and Hades were thrown into the lake of fire. This is the second death, the lake of fire. And if anyone's name was not found written in the book of life, he was thrown into the lake of fire."*

The Lake of Fire is a place of forever suffering.

When an unbeliever dies, he goes immediately to this terrible place called Hades. The common experience in both the temporary location, Hades, and the ultimate place for the unsaved, the Lake of Fire, is physical pain.

Notice in Luke 16:24:

> *"And he cried and said, Father Abraham, have mercy on me, and send Lazarus, that he may dip the tip of his finger in water, and cool my tongue; for I am tormented in this flame."*

> *Wow...he did not ask for a cup of water nor*

a bottle of water. The rich ruler said, "if Lazarus could just dip his finger in water to cool his tongue."

Think about that...

The rich man says he is in agony because of the flames. Right now, those who die without Christ are in Hades awaiting their final judgment, the Great White Throne Judgment. And at that judgment, Hades will be emptied, and all the unsaved who have ever lived will stand before God.

And because their names are not written in the Lamb's Book of Life, they will be judged by their deeds. That is a choice they made in this life. On that day, every unbeliever will see that his works do not meet the standard of perfect righteousness that God requires and understand why he has been sentenced to the Lake of Fire.

Here is the basic truth everyone needs to understand: when we die, we immediately begin experiencing God's blessing or God's judgment. While it is true that at some future day, believers will change location from the third Heaven to the New Heaven, and unbelievers will also change location from Hades into the Lake of Fire, a change of location is not the same as a change of eternal destiny. Heaven and Hell are eternal choices. If you wait until you die to choose your destination, you will have waited one second too long. Hell and Heaven are forever choices.

Chapter 6

Getting Your House in Order[15]

2 Kings 20:1-6: *"In those days was Hezekiah sick unto death. And the prophet Isaiah the son of Amoz came to him, and said unto him, Thus saith the Lord,* **Set thine house in order***; for thou shalt die, and not live. ² Then he turned his face to the wall, and prayed unto the Lord, saying, ³ I beseech thee, O Lord, remember now how I have walked before thee in truth and with a perfect heart, and have done that which is good in thy sight. And Hezekiah wept sore. ⁴ And it came to pass, afore Isaiah was gone out into the middle court, that the word of the Lord came to him, saying, ⁵ Turn again, and tell Hezekiah the captain of my people, Thus saith the Lord, the God of David thy father, I have heard thy prayer, I have seen thy tears: behold, I will heal thee: on the third day thou shalt go up unto the house of the Lord. ⁶ And I will add unto thy days fifteen years; and I will deliver thee and this city out of the hand of the king of Assyria; and I will defend this city for mine own* *sake, and for my servant David's sake."*

Hezekiah was born in 739 BC and died in 687 BC; he was at the age of 52 when he died. The Lord sent the Prophet Isaiah to Hezekiah 15 years early to warn him to **get his house in order**, for his expiration date was at hand; he was about to die. Hezekiah cried out to the Lord, begging the Lord to extend his expiration date. The Lord granted him an additional grace period of 15 more years to live.

No one knows the day or the hour when they will take their last breath.

But we do know what it says in Hebrews 9:27:

"And as it is appointed unto men once to die, but after this the judgment."

Psalms 90:10: "The days of our years are threescore years and ten; and if by reason of strength they be fourscore years, yet is their strength labour and sorrow."

God wasn't promising that every person would live to be seventy or eighty; however, the psalmist was simply describing our normal human experience. Our times are in God's hands, and for some, our journeys on earth are much shorter. Jesus was crucified when He was still in His 30s.

The first martyr, Stephen, likewise was probably still a young man when he was put to death for his faith (see Acts 7). My very own grandson (Jay) died when he was just two years old.

The real point the psalmist was making is that no matter who we are, our time on earth is limited, we all have an expiration date, and someday death will overtake us. Death is a reality, and no one evades it—no matter how strong they are or how rich they are.

> *Hebrews 9:27; "And as it is appointed unto men once to die, but after this the judgment."*

But this leads us to two very important questions. First, how should we prepare for death?

People may spend years preparing for a career or advancing in their job and yet never take five minutes to think about eternity and what will happen to them when they die. Are you putting your faith in man or God?

The other question is this: how should we spend the days God has given us? Will we live for ourselves, or will we live for God? Put Christ first and make your days count for Him.

No matter your faith, if you are Muslim, Jewish, Buddhist, Hebrew Israelite, atheist, or Christian. The one thing we do have in common is we will all die. So, let's get our houses in order.

Preparing for Death

Things We Need to Get in Order Before Death

Salvation - means to be saved from peril. The Bible speaks of such peril as being saved from our sins and the resulting penalty of spiritual death and separation from God. Salvation is a one-time "event."

It is the act of preserving or the state of being preserved from harm—a person or thing that is the means of preserving from harm. Christianity deliverance by redemption from the power of sin and from the penalties ensuing from it. It does not relieve us from the presence of sin.

We need salvation so that we can truly live the way that God intended for us to live. It is impossible for a spiritually dead person to know God and trust in His Word.[16]

> *John 3:16: "For **God** so loved the world, that he gave his only Son, that whoever believes in him should not perish but have eternal life."*

The greatest **gift** of all is the **gift** of **salvation**, given out of the greatest love of all, by the greatest person of all, namely **God**. Faith is the **gift** we receive from **God**[17]

By having faith in Jesus, Christians believe they receive God's grace. This means they believe God has blessed them, which in turn gives them the strength to live a good Christian life. Ultimately, **salvation** from sin was the purpose of Jesus' life, death, and resurrection.[18]

Through Christ, we are saved from the penalty of sin but not from the presence of sin.

> *Joshua 24:14-15: ·Now therefore fear the Lord, and serve him in sincerity and in truth: and put away the gods which your fathers served on the other side of the flood, and in Egypt; and serve ye the Lord. [15] And if it seem evil unto you to serve the Lord, choose you this day whom ye will serve; whether the gods which your fathers served that were on the other side*

> *of the flood, or the gods of the Amorites, in whose land ye dwell: but as for me and my house, we will serve the Lord."*

In the text above, Joshua had to make a choice.

I, too, made that choice some thirty-plus years ago. I grew up in church, went to church at least three times a week, played the drums, participated in church plays, and was the son of a pastor. However, being in church does not make you a Christian any more than being in a garage makes you a car.

On November 17th, 1987, I was in jail, facing a death sentence (electric chair). One morning about 3:15 am, I was taking a shower, and this strange sensation came over me. In the back of my mind, I believed that one day I would surrender my life totally to the Lord, but I would always tell myself that I would do it tomorrow. Well, tomorrow will be today. I fell on my knees crying, surrendering my life to the Lord, and asked Him to Lord over my life. The Spirit of God was cleaning the inner man, and the water from the shower was cleaning the outer man (Thank you, Jesus).

You can read the full story in my first book, *Grace and Mercy: My Path to Redemption.*

Yes, I've had many ups and downs struggling with this new walk and life that Jesus had planned for me. But today, 34 years later,

I've been married to my wife Rosalind for 27 faithful years. We have seven children, eleven grandchildren, and two great-grandchildren. (What a mighty God we serve).

My wife and I work together in ministry (I Am

My Brother's Keeper Ministries). We minister in the local jail, prisons, schools, streets, and communities, changing the lives of tomorrow today. We've taught marriage classes, how to study the bible classes, etc., all the glory to God.

Today we own this verse, Galatians 2:20-21:

> "**We** *are crucified with Christ: nevertheless* **we** *live; yet not us, but Christ liveth in* **us**: *and the life which we now live in the flesh we live by the faith of the Son of God, who loved* **us**, *and gave himself for us. We do not frustrate the grace of God: for if righteousness come by the law, then Christ is dead in vain.*"

Today, if you choose to accept Jesus' plan of salvation, I would like to share the prayer of salvation with you. It does not matter what you did last year, last night, or a few minutes ago.
Jesus says in John 6:37-40:

> "*All that the Father giveth me shall come to me;* **and him that cometh to me I will in no wise cast out**. *For I came down from heaven, not to do mine own will, but the will of him that sent me. And this is the Father's will which hath sent me, that of all which he hath given me I should lose nothing, but should raise it up again at the last day.*

> "*And this is the will of him that sent me, that every one which seeth the Son, and believeth on him, may have everlasting life: and I will raise him up at the last day.*"

A salvation prayer, known by many Christians as a "Sinners Prayer," is a prayer one would say to repent from sin, ask God for forgiveness, confess belief in Jesus Christ, and accept him as Lord and Savior. Saying a salvation prayer is the first step in your relationship with God.

Let us pray: *"Lord Jesus, for too long, I've kept you out of my life. I know that I am a sinner and that I cannot save myself. No longer will I close the door when I hear you knocking. By faith, I gratefully receive your gift of salvation. I am ready to trust you as my Lord and Savior. Thank you, Lord Jesus, for coming to earth. I believe you are the Son of God who died on the cross for my sins and rose from the dead on the third day. Thank you for bearing my sins and giving me the gift of eternal life. I believe your words are true. Come into my heart, Lord Jesus, and be my Savior. Amen."*

If you prayed this prayer, we ask that you contact us or a local church and share with them your experience of saying this prayer. Prayerfully, they will assist you in your new growth in the Lord. Welcome to the body of Christ; we love you.

Chapter 7

Burial / Life Insurance / Wills

Hosea 4:6; "My people are destroyed for lack of knowledge: because thou hast rejected knowledge."

This text reminds us that death does not always give us a warning that it is coming. Even though many of us have experienced death before, we still refuse to get our houses in order. Today is a new day, and together we are going to do better now that we know better.

I have witnessed families often not having the funds to properly bury their loved ones. It's because many of us don't want to deal with death, so we end up allowing death to deal with us. Many times, we have to bury the breadwinner. How are we going to pay the bills? Life has to go on.

We get insurance on our homes, cars, and phones. It's not that hard to get insurance to bury a loved one. Our loved ones are far more important to us than any material item. I would like to share with you some information about getting burial insurance.

Burial / Life Insurance / Wills 51

Let's get started...

With so many types and plans out there, life insurance can seem confusing. Whole life insurance, term insurance, permanent life insurance, burial insurance — knowing the difference among these options can help you make informed purchasing and planning decisions. One way to get started is to break down commonly asked questions and define important terms. Then you can understand what life insurance is and choose which option is best for you and your family.[19]

Why Is It Called Life Insurance?

This is the first question I asked...

Often people see life insurance as an instrument intended to deal with the death of someone. However, the product is correctly labeled 'life' insurance because it affects the living. Depending on the product, it can serve multiple purposes.

Obviously, when a family loses an income earner, there is a need for income replacement due to that death. Various types of life insurance products will solve this issue, including term insurance. That being said, other circumstances in life can be addressed with a quality life insurance product.[20]

What is Life Insurance?[21]

Life insurance is a legally binding contract that guarantees a benefit upon your death to named beneficiaries in exchange for premiums you pay. Types of life insurance include Term, Whole Life insurance, and Preneed Funeral insurance.

- **Term life insurance** is purchased for a specific time period and protects your loved ones from income loss after your passing.
- **Whole Life insurance** is a type of permanent life insurance that covers you while you're alive for as long as you pay your premiums. A whole life insurance policy won't expire after a certain term.
- **Preneed**—Funeral Insurance specifically helps cover your funeral expenses. You pre-plan arrangements directly with a funeral home to lessen the burden on loved ones to pay for and coordinate a memorial service during an already difficult time.

Banking / Saving Accounts

There are many types of savings and investment accounts that you can designate for your life insurance purposes. This will allow you to have full control of your account.

Let's educate ourselves. It does not matter what your beliefs are; we will all experience the death of a loved one. Let's not continue to avoid facing this matter; let's get ahead of it. So, when that time comes (and it will), we can freely process grieving and mourning of our loss.

What Is a Will and Why Do I Need One?[22]

I have witnessed many families split at a time of grieving because there were no wills in place to answer the question of what the dead or dying loved one's wishes were. I witnessed firsthand physical fights over whether a loved one should be taken off life support, who should be in charge of the affairs of the funeral, how to divide the loved one's remaining assets, and the list goes on. I have also lost a student who was killed by another family member because of a family dispute at the funeral.

A will is a legal document that sets forth your wishes regarding the distribution of your properties and the care of any minor children. If you die without a will, those wishes may not be carried out. Further, your heirs may be forced to spend additional time, money, and emotional energy to settle your affairs after you're gone.

Wills can vary in their effectiveness, depending on the type, though no document will likely resolve every issue that arises after your death. Here's what you need to know about these vital documents.

KEY TAKEAWAYS[23]

- A will is a legal document that spells out your wishes regarding the care of your children, as well as the distribution of your assets after your death.
- Failure to prepare a will typically leaves decisions about your estate in the hands of judges or state officials and may also cause family strife.
- You can prepare a valid will yourself, but you should have the document witnessed to decrease the likelihood of successful challenges later.
- To be completely sure everything is in order, consider having your will prepared by

a trusts and estates attorney

Why You Should Have a Will[24]

Some people think that only the very wealthy or those with complicated assets need wills. However, there are many good reasons to have a will.

- You can be clear about who gets your assets. You can decide who gets what and how much.
- You can keep your assets out of the hands of people you don't want to have them (like an estranged relative).
- You can identify who should care for your children. Without a will, the courts will decide.
- Your heirs will have a faster and easier time getting access to your assets.
- You can plan to save your estate money on taxes. You can also give gifts and charitable donations, which can help offset the estate tax.

A Written, Witnessed Will Is Best[25]

To maximize the likelihood that your wishes will be carried out, create what's known as a <u>testamentary will</u>. This is the most familiar type of will; you prepare the document and then sign it in the presence of witnesses. It's arguably the best insurance against successful challenges to your wishes by family members or business associates after you die. You can write one yourself, but for greater insurance, have it prepared by a trusts and estates attorney.

Matthew 24:42-44; "Watch therefore: for

*ye know not what hour your Lord doth come.*⁴³ *But know this, that if the goodman of the house had known in what watch the thief would come, he would have watched, and would not have suffered his house to be broken up.*⁴⁴ *Therefore be ye also ready: for in such an hour as ye think not the Son of man cometh."*

My Personal Experience of Writing My Own Will

My wife and I wrote our wills many years ago. While writing this book, we have had to go back and make some adjustments.

The Lord asked me to write a letter to my family that would be read during my funeral. I knew that I would have to do it, but I struggled for two weeks. Finally, one night, I could not get to sleep. I went into my office about 2:30 am and said, "Ok Lord, let's do this." It was the most challenging letter that I have ever written in my life. I felt an out-of-the-body experience; I was there at my service as this letter was read. It was filled with pain, humor, and praise. When I returned to reality, it was now 5:45 am. In those three hours and fifteen minutes, I had only written a page. But it was the most fearful yet fulfilling moment of my life. I have come very close to death several times in my life, but this was the first time that I *saw* death. The sting of death really has been removed, and I now have the victory over death.

Chapter 8

Passing The Mantle to Your Successor[26]

Deuteronomy 31:1-2; "And Moses went and spake these words unto all Israel.² And he said unto them, I am an hundred and twenty years old this day; I can no more go out and come in: also the Lord hath said unto me, Thou shalt not go over this Jordan."

Deuteronomy 31:7-8; "And Moses called unto Joshua, and said unto him in the sight of all Israel, Be strong and of a good courage: for thou must go with this people unto the land which the Lord hath sworn unto their fathers to give them; and thou shalt cause them to inherit it.⁸ And the Lord, he it is that doth go before thee; he will be with thee, he will not fail thee, neither forsake thee: fear not, neither be dismayed."

Moses knew that his days were numbered. So, while Moses was alive, he began to prepare his successor, Joshua. Most families don't usually appoint a leader over that generation; it often falls into play by an individual's character and gifts.

While it's certainly human nature to focus on the here and now—relegating the future to the back burner—when it comes to operating a family successfully over the long term, it's critical for leaders to choose and groom their successors.

The fact is, the more valuable a leader is to his or her family, the less valuable the family is. It may not always be a designated individual; generations can be prepared and groomed to respond to an unplanned event such as death, disability, divorce, etc.

Family leaders owe it to their family members to not just choose an heir apparent but to help that person/generation adopt a leadership role before the transition takes place.

This is especially important when the successor is significantly younger than the individual whose shoes he or she will fill; in those cases, it's even more critical for leaders to take steps to ensure their family members gain confidence in their successors.

In family matters, when it is an adult child who needs to be elevated in the eyes of the family as a worthy successor, leaders need to ensure their behavior is professional and doesn't reflect the child-parent relationship. That means not being patronizing in either actions or tone of voice during public interaction.

When a successor has been adequately prepared, there will be limited or no disruption when that person takes the reins—as both successor and family members will have had a chance to see the "new blood's" competence in action.

Different Roles

In most homes, there are those who are set in their roles and their roles only. We must invest the time to learn one another's roles. One may take care of the needs outside the home (breadwinner), and another may take care of all the interior needs (heart) of the family (washing, cooking, bills, kids' needs, etc.)

What happens if one dies and leaves that big void of keeping the family functioning.

- The person that takes care of the interior needs to have a backup plan where they have some knowledge and training in getting into the work field. Remember, if we don't make plans for these days, we will be up the creek without a paddle. So, let's have these conversations while there is still time.
- The person that works outside of the home needs to know all of what is done in the interior of the home. They need to sit down together and go over all the finances, budgeting, bills, needs of the children, cooking, etc.
- Too often, we are only concerned with our individual roles and think very little about the other person's role. Remember, it's not if we die; we will die one day, and we do not know the order of our deaths. So, let's use the time we have now and have these hard discussions so we can work out a plan before we are faced with the loss of a loved one.

If you are a single person and you are fulfilling both roles, you need to seek someone to who you can pass the mantle. This is something that must also be a part of your will. *Let's get our houses in order today, for there might not be a tomorrow.*

Chapter 9

Pre-Planning Your Funeral[27]

<u>Pre-planning your funeral</u> arrangements can take some of the logistical and financial stresses off of your family after your death and ensure that you get the kind of funeral you want. Don't feel pressured to plan it down to the last detail. While some have no problem planning their own funeral, it's understandable if you find it too difficult or overwhelming. However, you can still let your family know a few aspects to make it much smoother for everyone involved.

The Biggest Decision You Should Make: Burial, Cremation, or Donation?

First and foremost: Let your family and loved ones know if you want to be buried or cremated. Or you can put it in your Will or a letter to your family. Just let someone know your definitive answer to avoid any unnecessary stress during an already emotional time. If you don't care, let them know that too.

If you choose burial, you need to purchase a

burial plot or a spot in a mausoleum at a cemetery.

If you choose cremation, you can decide what you want to be done with the cremated remains, including burial, scattering, or giving them to friends and family members to be stored in an urn.

Keep The Body, Donate the Usable Parts

If you want to help others but still want your family to bury or cremate your body, you can simply donate your organs. Next time you renew your driver's license, select the box that says, "organ donor." Make sure you do your research.

Finding A Funeral Director

Engage the services of a funeral home you trust and like and work with their funeral director to plan your burial or cremation and funeral or memorial service. The funeral director can also help you purchase any goods and services you'll need for the burial, cremation, funeral, or memorial service.

If you're planning a funeral followed by burial, you will typically work with a funeral director at a funeral home. They will help you with all the arrangements, including working with a cemetery to purchase a plot and orchestrate the burial.

If you are planning a funeral followed by cremation, you will typically work with a funeral director at a funeral home. They will help you connect with a crematory to arrange the cremation.

If you are planning a direct cremation followed by a memorial service or ash scattering, you may be able to work with the crematory directly—you don't have to work with a funeral home

How Are You Paying For The Funeral?

When making pre-arrangements, it's common to pre-pay for some or all of the products and services you're organizing.

There are a number of ways to pay for pre-arrangements, and some may meet your needs better than others.

Cemetery Arrangements

You can work with a funeral home to find a cemetery or approach a cemetery directly and have a funeral director coordinate the arrangements. Here are a few things you need to consider:

- <u>Find a cemetery</u>: Location, religion, and environment are the big factors to consider when choosing a cemetery, as is vacancy (not just for the immediate burial, but for future family members as well).
- <u>Decide if you want multiple plots</u>: Are you buying plots for the future as well? If you are, you'll want to find plots or mausoleum spaces that are together.
- <u>Visit the cemetery</u>: Take a look at the grounds: are they well maintained? Inspect the plot you're buying: is it what you had in mind? Take this opportunity to ask any questions you might have before you sign the paperwork. Someone else can visit the cemetery on your behalf if you cannot visit yourself.

Cremation and Burial Products

Caskets come in a variety of styles and prices, and the selection of a casket is a personal choice. You can purchase a casket from the funeral home or from an online retailer.

Burial Vault/Grave Liner

The cemetery will likely require a burial vault or grave liner, and the funeral home may have a limited selection of vaults and liners, so be aware that you may not have much of a choice for this product.

Urn

Cremation urns come in a variety of styles and prices, and the selection of an urn is a personal choice.

Cremation Casket

The selection of a cremation casket is a personal choice. You may purchase a casket for the funeral service that is then used for the cremation, though the casket should be made without metal as metal cannot be cremated. If you don't want to buy a casket, but you want to use one for the funeral service, you may rent one from the funeral home for the funeral service and use an alternative container for the cremation.

Tip

Save all receipts for all funeral-related purchases. These expenses may be deductible on future tax returns.

Have You Made Any Arrangements Already?

Have you made any previous arrangements? You'd probably remember. Has someone already made these purchases on your behalf? Sometimes family members have plots set aside. Ask around to make sure. If someone did you the kindness of purchasing a plot, share those details with your loved ones to avoid confusion and the purchase of another plot.

What Type of Service Do You Want?

Funerals, graveside services, and memorial services are the most common types, though you can also have a funeral service in your own home.

There are also other events you may want, like wakes, viewings, and visitations. These are sometimes held before the service, and gatherings or receptions are often held after the service. Other things to consider:
- Choosing a location for the service
- Deciding who you would like to serve as pallbearers
- Selecting readings and songs you'd like to have performed at the service
- Who will do the eulogy (a speech or writing that acknowledges who has just died).
- Eulogies are often done by family members, friends, clergy, or funeral conductors.

Personalize Your Funeral or Memorial Service

You may consider identifying desired participants, readings, and even decorations if you wish.

Other things to consider:

Choose a Location

Funerals are typically held at funeral homes, religious places of worship, chapels at cemeteries, or at gravesites.

Choose an Officiant

If you are having the service at a place of worship, the religious leader there will likely lead the service. Otherwise, anyone you choose can lead the service.

Choose Participants

There are many ways for friends and family to participate in a funeral or memorial service. Identify who you'd like to serve as pallbearers and deliver eulogies and other readings.

Participants may also sing songs, play music, or offer other tributes.

Make a list of guests to invite

If there are specific people you would like to have invited to the service, write down their names and contact information so that the person managing the service will be sure to invite them.

Design other elements of your funeral or memorial service

Let your family know how you'd like the service to look and feel. Choose flowers, music, and other personal touches.

Things To Consider

The above information are things to consider

before you wake up one morning and you are faced with making these decisions. Planning for a funeral can be very challenging at any point in life. It can be overwhelming when having to make these decisions when we are grieving the loss of a loved one and are dealing with a limited amount of time to make these decisions.

Chapter 10

Coping With the Loss of Your Loved One

Losing a loved one introduces you to a pain that will never show up on any X-ray, C-T Scan, MRI, or any doctor's exam. It's a pain that you can not truly touch or feel.

I've been shot and stabbed. I have fallen from a two-story building, broken six ribs, punctured my lungs, broke several bones in my spine, suffered several cases of kidney stones, suffered from a sciatic nerve, and had my heart broken as a teenager.

None of these pains compare to the pain I suffered when I lost my two-year-old grandson. This pain could not be located in any particular area of the body. It had an effect on all of my body parts at the same time.

Many people are able to move on but do not know the hidden damage that was done to their inner being. Some people are so damaged that they are not able to function with a normal life at all. I have learned that this is not a pain you get over, but you can learn how to cope with this pain.

The Bible says in Hosea 4:6 that "my people perish for a lack of knowledge." I would like to give you some information about coping skills and the need to get some professional and spiritual help. We need to get help in this area just as we would if we got hit by a car.

> *Deuteronomy 34:8; And the children of Israel wept for Moses in the plains of Moab thirty days: so the days of weeping and mourning for Moses were ended.*

In the above text, God set aside time for His people to mourn and grieve. We, too, must follow God's plan and take the necessary time to process our mourning and grieving. In that time, we must seek the spiritual and professional help we need.

Coping With the Loss of a Loved One[28]

Coping with the loss of a close friend or family member may be one of the hardest challenges that many of us face. When we lose a spouse, sibling, or parent, our grief can be particularly intense. Loss is understood as a natural part of life, but we can still be overcome by shock and confusion, leading to prolonged periods of sadness or depression. The sadness typically diminishes in intensity as time passes, but grieving is an important process in order to cope with these feelings and continue to embrace the time you had with your loved one.

Everyone reacts differently to death and employs personal coping mechanisms for grief. Research shows that some people can recover from loss on their own through the passage of time if they have <u>social support and healthy habits</u>. It may take months or years to come to terms with a loss. There is no "normal" time period for someone to grieve.

Don't expect to pass through phases of grief either, as research suggests that most people do not go through stages as progressive steps.

If your relationship with the deceased was difficult, this will also add another dimension to the grieving process. It may take some time and thought before you are able to look back on the relationship and adjust to the loss.

Human beings are naturally resilient, considering some of us can endure loss and then continue on with our own lives. But some people may struggle with grief for longer periods of time and feel unable to carry out daily activities.

Individuals with severe grief or complicated grief could benefit from the help of a psychologist or another licensed mental health professional with a specialization in grief.

How Do I Move on With Life?

Mourning the loss of a close friend or relative takes time, but research tells us that it can also be the catalyst for a renewed sense of meaning that offers purpose and direction to life. Grieving individuals may find it helpful to use some of the following strategies to help them process and come to terms with loss:

Talk about the death of your loved one with friends or colleagues in order to help you understand what happened and remember your friend or family member. Avoidance can lead to isolation and will disrupt the healing process with your support systems.

- Accept your feelings. You may experience a wide range of emotions from sadness, anger, or even exhaustion. All of these feelings are normal, and it's important to recognize when you are feeling this way. If you feel stuck or overwhelmed by these emotions, it may be helpful to talk with a spiritual advisor, a licensed psychologist, or another mental health professional who can help you cope with your feelings and find ways to get back on track.
- Take care of yourself and your family. Eating healthy foods, exercising, and getting plenty of sleep can help your physical and emotional health. The grieving process can take a toll on one's body.
- Make sure you check in with your loved ones and that they are taking the necessary healthy steps to maintain their health.
- Reach out and help others dealing with the loss. Spending time with loved ones of the deceased can help everyone cope. Whether it's sharing stories or listening to your loved one's favorite music, these small efforts can make a big difference to some. Helping others has the added benefit of making you feel better as well.
- Remember and celebrate the lives of your

loved ones. Anniversaries of a lost loved one can be a difficult time for friends and family, but they can also be a time for remembrance and honoring them. It may be that you decide to collect donations to a favorite charity of the deceased, pass on a family name to a baby, or plant a garden in memory.
- What you choose is up to you, as long as it allows you to honor that unique relationship in a way that feels right to you.

How Psychologists Can Help

Psychologists are trained to help people better handle the fear, guilt, or anxiety that can be associated with the death of a loved one. If you need help dealing with your grief or managing a loss, consult with a psychologist or other licensed mental health professional. Psychologists can help people build their resilience and develop strategies to get through their sadness. Practicing psychologists use a variety of evidence-based treatments — most commonly psychotherapy (talk therapy) — to help people improve their lives.

Psychologists, who have doctoral degrees, receive one of the highest levels of education of any health care professional.

How Christian Based Grief Counseling Helps[29]

As you mourn your loved one's death, a Christian counselor will help you understand that there is life after death.

The goal of the Christian counselor is to help

guide you through the grieving process and to help you understand if your loved one was saved, they are in the loving arms of the Heavenly Father. This enlightenment serves to bring you peace and acceptance. It also helps you get your spiritual house in order.

Ways to Cope

Communication is one of the best ways to cope with the loss of a loved one. You may want to speak with someone who is close to you. You may want to speak to God through prayer. You may want to write down how you feel. Expressing your feelings through some form of communication about the loss you have suffered and the grief that you feel can eventually help you find comfort.

Living a Godly Life

Once you find comfort and acceptance, the grief counselor will work with you to help you move on with your Christian life. This will enable you to someday join your loved one in heaven. You will learn about God's plan for you now that your loved one is gone. Along with your counselor, you will devise a plan on how to make the most of your life. This may include spreading the Word of God, helping others who are in need or doing charitable work.

If your loved one was not saved, your counselor can help you as well in that area. And if you are not saved, this would be a great time for you to give your life to the Lord.

Moving On

Therapy sessions may come to an end at some point once you feel at peace with your loved one's death and empowered to proceed with your life in the glory of God.

> *Luke 22:31-32; "And the Lord said, Simon, Simon, behold, Satan hath desired to have you, that he may sift you as wheat: But I have prayed for thee, that thy faith fail not: and when thou art converted, strengthen thy brethren."*

Once we are converted, we are then able to reach back and be of support to others who are going through.

Stories Of Those Who Have Lost Loved Ones

Below is a group of people sharing their personal stories of how they are coping with the loss of their loved one. I am sure you will be able to relate to some of these stories as you reflect on your own personal story.

The Loss of a Father

After my father passed on my birthday, May 9, 2014, a part of me left with him. I used to write music and sing a lot, but ever since then, I haven't sung as much and really haven't written a song, but I still sing to the Lord. One way I coped was to be sincerely honest with God about my feelings; this was expressed through anger and tears. But I eventually had to accept this as God's will and timing. I created a new infatuation with old-

school music that my dad listened to as a way to hold memories of him in my heart. I've saved songs that were some of his favorites; sometimes I cry when I hear them, other times it's sweet enjoyment.
Antoine Thurston

The Loss of a Grandmother

I lost my grandmother while incarcerated. I was devastated, to say the least. My grandmother was very dear to my heart. She was such a pillar of strength and very kindhearted. I've had so much time to process the loss as well as the emptiness I felt at that time. I realize I had a lot of regrets, namely her witnessing my actions as a result of my addiction. Her last words to me were that she wanted me to change my life. My main regret is she didn't get to see that happen, and she has never met her grandchildren. But after all that has happened, I am assured she is looking down from heaven cheering me on (I miss her so much).
Rosalind Smith

The Loss of a Grandson by Suicide

My most cherished blessings are the memories of my grandson Josh that lives in my heart every day! He was energetic, smart, and a beautiful child. As a young adult, he was kind, thoughtful, and aware of the world that surrounded him in his short life. Josh accepted life's experiences and always had a smile on his handsome face and was non-judgmental if he experienced disappointment. Josh's most endearing quality was his spiritual thoughts and ideas that he shared with me. His desire was for all people to be able to live in unity and peace. I miss our quiet time together.

Josh's sudden departure from my life was devastating! I wanted to be alone in my sorrow. I slept in his room. I continuously looked at his pictures. I printed and framed my favorites that reminded me of the happy times of our life together! Eventually, I passed on Josh's possessions that he enjoyed. I felt Josh would have wanted his friends to enjoy the things that helped to make his life rich.

They say that God abhors a vacuum, and when one door closes, another door opens. Josh's cat Tigger gets more of my attention now and fills my day with joy. He is the mutual link that connects me with Josh.

It is heartwarming to visit Josh's resting place. His name is on the marker where I know he is resting in peace. I believe that God called him home in his young life because he had a higher purpose for him. It has been almost three years since Josh left our earth and walked into eternity. I know he is in God's care. I am so honored to have been Josh's oma.

Barbara Railsback

The Loss of a Two-Year-Old Son

I lost my son, Jaymerson, at the age of two, in an unfortunate, unexpected daycare accident. That day will forever be an unwanted memory that never goes away. Rightfully, I was not prepared to lose a child. I know that we've all heard the saying that children should bury their parents, so it was unnatural for me to have my child transition before me at such a young age and so tragically. I was immediately thrust into something I had never had to deal with before; the grief, the funeral planning, and all that comes with the death of a loved one. That entire period felt as though it was a horrible dream that I could not wake from.

I endured the pain of bringing him into the world, but of course, that was expected. The pain of childbirth comes with many ways to cope, but this, the loss of my child, was a completely different loss. This was a loss that did not come with a set of standard ways to cope. The pain of losing him did not come close to measuring up to the pain I endured bringing him into this world. I had at least nine months to plan for his arrival, to get everything necessary for the first few months of his life. I had a year to plan for his first birthday. Then another for his second. It was simple by the time he got here. I had already had two other boys who were eleven and ten at the time of Jay's arrival, so I was prepared for that.

What I wasn't prepared for was having to choose a small box to lay my baby boy in, having to buy his last pair of pants, last shirt, and pair of socks. I was not prepared for a forever goodbye. He had only been with me for two years and four months. However, the painful reality was that my baby boy, my Jay, was gone and was never coming back. He hadn't gone to his dad's for the weekend. It was hard to accept the fact that there would no longer be sounds of his little feet running throughout the house. I would no longer hear his infectious little laugh.

I had no clue on how to prepare for him leaving me. There was no way to even imagine how I could cope. How was I supposed to cope with losing my baby boy? I didn't even know how to grieve, how to even accept the fact that this was even happening to me. Before losing my son, I didn't know there were steps to grieving, but subconsciously, I had experienced each step. I still feel like I was dreaming. There were days I waited on his dad to pull up with him in the back seat. I would try to sleep, praying that I would be awakened by him jumping on the bed. I could not make myself believe that I would never ever touch my baby again (Denial). I was so angry at the staff that was employed at that daycare. I wanted them to hurt. I wanted to burn that place down, during work hours or after. I did not care. I was angry at myself for taking him that morning. I was angry with the families of the children that were spared that day. I was angry at the children. Lord knows I wouldn't wish this on anyone else, but I'd rather it had been some other child than mine (Anger).

My family and I had been waiting in the hospital chapel, where we were being updated on my son's progress. I wasn't ready when the doctor came in and spoke words to me that I'd only ever heard uttered on television: "I'm sorry, ma'am, we did all that we could do." Before that moment, I prayed to God like never before, "Lord, please let my baby be ok. I don't care if I have to change his diaper for the rest of his life; just let him live!" and that was my actual prayer (Bargaining).

At this point, I didn't have the courage to burn the daycare down. Nor did I want the other families and kids to feel this same hurt. I still didn't know how to cope with what I was faced with. I had two other kids to be there for, and I didn't know how to be there for them or there for myself. I felt hopeless. I didn't know how to not hurt anymore. I fell into a deep depression. I didn't eat, and I cried constantly. I didn't get out of bed; family members had to force me to do simple things, like shower. To this day, I couldn't tell you how my two older boys were coping. I couldn't do much of anything, and I didn't know much of anything. What I did know and what I would've been willing to do was not live anymore (Depression).

The last step of the grieving process was and still is the hardest, yet it is the most important. Learning to accept, in a sense, was life or death. However, leaving my boys without a mom was not an option. Up until now, it had been only by God's grace and mercy that allowed me to function from day to day. I began to pray for strength, but I couldn't get to where I needed to be with prayer alone. Before this point, I had never considered seeing a therapist. I was a little apprehensive, but I knew it had to be done. My therapist taught me a few different coping mechanisms that have helped and still do help me. At one point, I couldn't talk about it without breaking down and shutting down, but she taught me that talking about what had happened was helpful and good for me. Journaling and/or writing letters to Jay also was something that I picked up that helped me. These tools were very helpful initially in my coping process.

It has been 15 years since the accident, and

I no longer resist the reality of what happened. I still miss him until my heart aches. I have days where I think of him, and my crying is uncontrollable. I've realized that pain will always be there and a part of me. Now a quick aside—I always thought going through the grieving process would lead me to acceptance, and I would just stay there. I've learned that grief is a fluid process and that it doesn't always happen in the order listed. Many times, I've revisited all of the stages. Now that many years have passed, new things hurt. As I see other kids reach milestones, I often wonder what he would be doing at this age. What type of student would he be? Would he have played sports? He'd be preparing to turn 17 years old this year. These thoughts constantly flood my mind. It definitely hurts because these are questions I'll never have answers for. When I have these thoughts, it causes me to again slip back into a dark place. That is when I use the tools I learned over the years.

I now know that instead of allowing the darkness to envelope me, I have to do other things. So now I go to the gym and sweat out all of those emotions. I call one of my now-adult sons so that we can talk and reminisce on the good memories. I have accepted that I will forever have my sad moments and that grief is a constant process. The denial, anger, and depression still arise, but I can't allow them to take my peace. There is no particular time schedule for these things, and no two people grieve the same. I can admit I still battle with depression and my days are not always bright. But in the midst of that, I continue to pray to God for strength. I stay in therapy, and I have an amazing support system. I recognize the tools and when to utilize them. They have helped me in this process over all these years and the years to come and allowed me to cope with my son's demise.

Kim

The Loss of a Mother

My mother's passing was a cumulative pool of grief and emotional toil. My mother didn't raise me beyond ten years old, so we never cultivated a healthy or nurturing mother-daughter relationship over the years. My father was the biggest influence in my life as a child and even into my adulthood.

Over the years, I tried reaching out to her, and we just never grew relationally the way I hoped, so that wish never came to fruition.

My mom had resentment for my dad after their divorce, and I felt she sometimes took it out on my brother and me. And at a low point in her life, she even insulted me and told me I would never amount to anything in life. Those words cut deep but became my fuel to succeed in life and to be the best mother God created me to be.

As my mom lay on her deathbed, with only days to live, we never had "that final conversation" about life or our relationship. I don't know why it never transpired. Maybe it was me or her avoiding the conversation, or just the circumstances of so many loved ones passing in and out of her room. Consequently, I never had closure with my mom before she died.

Even though I wasn't close to my mother, I still felt called to be by her side and advocate for her comfort and dignity until her final day. I wanted her to know she was loved and not alone on her final journey here on Earth. I was in her room with one of my sisters when she took her final breath.

As we prepared for her funeral, I observed how others were grieving for the loss of my mom. I, however, was not lamenting over her being gone since I knew she was in the arms of Jesus. I was mourning the relationship we never had. We didn't talk on a regular basis; she missed my wedding, the birth of my son, and so many other milestones in my life. The memories or daily habits with her included were not there to miss.

God often reminds me that my mother's childhood plays a prodigious role in how she handled parenting. It helps me forgive her and have compassion for her own trials and tribulations she endured. And this is where I turn my own poignant emotions to Jesus. I know it is only in Him will I find comfort, hope, love, joy, and restoration. The Bible says in Joel 2:25, "So I will restore to you the years that the swarming locust has eaten." God has a way of restoring more than just physical things, for I have seen it a multitude of times. So one day, I may encounter my mom in heaven, and the grief and toil will be replaced with rejoicing and unspeakable joy.

My Journey of Loss
Soyna Milu

The Loss of a Boyfriend by Suicide

Boom! Boom! is what I heard at the door the night my life changed forever. Nothing could prepare me for the sight, the aftermath, and the feel of defeat that I now have to deal with. I am a firm believer in God and that everything happens for a reason, but that moment is when I needed God to wrap around me the most.

For you to understand my after-death experience of losing a loved one, I would need you to understand what I was dealing with before his suicide. God revealed to me in 2014 that I was going to die from a gunshot to the head by my boyfriend in the very house that he died in. Before my mom died, she had the same dream. I thought that I could fix this by making sure I showed love and embraced him more every day. Changing a situation meant that I had the power to be God, which I am not. I tried to build up a person that truthfully was already broken from the beginning. I was always strong and felt that my strength was powerful enough to help the most troubled. Never leave family behind, but truthfully, I did not understand the magnitude of the situation. All I could see was this is the love of my life and we could get through this. Love is sometimes beauty and pain.

A month prior, God told me to tell someone. I had no clue that I was going to need her, that a storm was coming and that she was someone I needed. When that moment came, I was screaming on the sidewalk, and she was the only person I wanted to talk to, well, besides running at full speed and never stopping. My family did not allow me to hold him, and I was angry because he sat in the middle of the front yard for hours alone before anyone would even touch him. Hours before this happened, I was getting bad feelings, so I prayed with my children. I wanted them to sleep so I could go outside to check on him.

In the midst of praying, I went into a deep sleep. While people were trying to help him right outside my window, I was asleep like a baby. God shielded my children that night and me, too.

See, we can plan our lives the way we want, but God has a purpose beyond the mind of the flesh. Every day I am picking up pieces of my life even when I do not want to. I had to break the news to two beautiful children that their father had died. The questions and the anger they feel from him not being here are what I have to piece together. My son loves talking about his father and making up stories about him and what they did together.

My way of coping is by moving along, but I can't because their father is their hero. I have to keep a secret about how he died because they aren't capable of understanding right now. I get angry sometimes because now I am a single mother raising two kids, and I know how people get treated when they are single mothers. I started remodeling the house because I needed a fresh start, but it did not heal me; it put a Band-Aid on the pain. We are like a favorite coffee mug that just shattered unexpectedly that you try to put back together, but it will never look the same. I treat each day as a new day, starting my life over in a brand-new book. My fear is telling my kids, and they feel that it is okay to do something. The trend now, to me, is glorifying suicide. I understand that they want to bring awareness, but I dislike the way. Awareness is what is needed because all the signs were there, but I never dealt with someone like that, and I always thought *not in this family*. He never said he was battling anything; I had to always look into his eyes to see his feelings.

See, the after-death is not just for the people that died; it is for the people left behind. It is how they continue to survive, how they cope with their new form of reality, what changes they make for the better. See, I want my daughter to be a psychologist so she can help the minds of others heal. I want my son to be a successful contractor or engineer that owns it all because his father was good with his hands.

With me, I am in the process of starting a foundation that gives scholarships to families who have been impacted by suicide at my alma mater. See, I wouldn't have been successful in my career without him. It hurts because the two very people that helped me get to this point and cared for my children are no longer here. Life is what you make it despite your circumstances. I just chose to make it positive through the help of GOD. To be truthful, God has since opened so many doors for me because I chose to still follow him and make peace with God's decision. My daughter said, "Well, why did God take my daddy so young?" My response is, "Because sometimes God has a place where pain is not a factor, and the work for them is completed." I am more than an accountant; my job is to be an accountant and make good money, but my purpose is to give hope and a chance to children who do not have a chance at life, chances that he never had but wanted. A mind to see the beauty in the midst of hopelessness. It's all a state of mind. Which one will you choose?

Ky E

Final Words

First of all, I would like to thank God and all of you who helped me make this much-needed book of information possible.

I want to thank those who sacrifice themselves to revisit those painful times in sharing the loss of their loved ones, inviting us to experience the darkest times of their lives and how they are coping with their losses. Thank you.

Thank all of you who took time out of your busy schedules to write forewords to this book that God inspired me to pen. God used all of you in different seasons of my life in helping me to become the man of God that I am today. Thank you.

Thanks to all of you who have invested in the purchase of this book. We pray that this information will help you in making the necessary decisions for you and your family. We pray that the information in this book lightens your load during your mourning and grieving moments. Thank you.

I want to thank Dr. Antoine Thurston for reading over all the scripture, making sure that everything was in line. Thank You

I want to thank my publisher, Mr. Jones and company (Dove Publishing). Mr. Jones has been very instrumental in my short writing career. He walked me through every step of my first book "Grace and Mercy." They later published my wife's book "My Path to Praise." And here we are again with my second book, *"After Death, Then What? Preparing to Die."* Thank you.

The first shall be last and the last shall be first. I want to thank my wife for making it possible for me to have the time to do all the research for this book. My wife is my teacher, helper, lover, and friend. Out of all the people in this world, I thank God for having me in mind when He brought her into this world. I love you, honey.

Thank You…

Endnotes

1   "Death & Dying." What Is Death | Death and Dying, http://www.death-and-dying.org/what-is-death.htm/.

2   ibid

3   "Thanatology: What Is Life? When Is Death?" Time, Time Inc., 27 May 1966, http://content.time.com/time/subscriber/article/0,33009,835670,00.html.

4   Are the Dead, Really Dead - What Is Death?, https://www.preparingforeternity.com/dead.htm.

5   Portions of this section excerpted from "Where Do Christians Go When They Die?" Pathway to Victory, 9 Oct. 2019, https://ptv.org/devotional/where-do-christians-go-when-they-die/.

6   Ibid

7   Portions of this section excerpted from "Does Islam Believe in Hell?" Owlcation, Owlcation, 9 Dec. 2015, https://owlcation.com/humanities/Islam-and-Hell-Does-Islam-Believe-In-Hell.

8   Ibid

9   Ibid

10   Ibid

11   Ibid

12   Taylor, Justin "The 11 Beliefs You Should Know about Jehovah's Witnesses When They Knock at the Door." The Gospel Coalition, 17 Aug. 2017, https://www.thegospelcoalition.org/blogs/justin-taylor/the-11-beliefs-you-should-know-about-jehovahs-witnesses-when-they-knock-at-the-door/.

13   Portions in this section excerpted from "Press

Reports Quote Adventist View of Hell." Adventist News Network, General Conference, 12 Oct. 1998, https://adventist.news/news/press-reports-quote-adventist-view-of-hell.

14   Portions in this section excerpted from "Where Do Unbelievers Go When They Die?" Pathway to Victory, 11 Oct. 2019, https://ptv.org/devotional/where-do-unbelievers-go-when-they-die/.

15   Portions in this section excerpted from "Does the Bible Say Somewhere That God Has Promised to Give Us 70 Years of Life?" Billy Graham Evangelistic Association, 7 Aug. 2014, https://billygraham.org/answer/does-the-bible-say-somewhere-that-god-has-promised-to-give-us-70-years-of-life/.

16   "Why Do We Need Salvation?" Biblword.net, 1 Feb. 2021, https://www.biblword.net/why-do-we-need-salvation/.

17   "What Does Salvation Mean in Christianity." Christianity, 21 Nov. 2020, https://www.sorrowandblood.com/faq/what-does-salvation-mean-in-christianity.html.

18   Wilcox, Manon. "What Is the Main Point of Salvation by Langston Hughes?" Colors, https://colors-newyork.com/what-is-the-main-point-of-salvation-by-langston-hughes/.

19   "What Is Life Insurance? A Quick and Simple Guide." GWIC, https://gwic.com/Education-Center/Life-Insurance-101/What-Is-Life-Insurance-A-Quick-and-Simple-Guide.

20   "Why Call It Life Insurance?" Why Call It Life Insurance? | First Heartland, https://www.firstheartland.com/blog/why-call-it-life-insurance.

21   Portions in this section excerpted from "What Is Life Insurance? A Quick and Simple Guide." GWIC, https://gwic.com/Education-Center/Life-

Insurance-101/What-Is-Life-Insurance-A-Quick-and-Simple-Guide.

22   Portions in this section excerpted from Smith, Lisa. "What Is a Will and Why Do I Need One Now?" Investopedia, Investopedia, 22 Oct. 2021, https://www.investopedia.com/articles/pf/08/what-is-a-will.asp.

23   Ibid

24   Ibid

25   Ibid

26   Portions in this section excerpted from "The Process of Preparing a Successor." Family Business Consulting in Tampa, FL, 3 Nov. 2020, https://federerperformance.com/2014/12/10/process-preparing-successor/.

27   This chapter excerpted from "How to Pre-Plan Your Funeral." Everplans, https://www.everplans.com/articles/how-to-pre-plan-your-funeral.

28   Portions of this section excerpted from "Grief: Coping with the Loss of Your Loved One." American Psychological Association, American Psychological Association, https://www.apa.org/topics/families/grief.

29   Hardy, Marcelina. "Christian Grief Counseling." LoveToKnow, LoveToKnow Media, https://dying.lovetoknow.com/Christian_Grief_Counseling.

www.ingramcontent.com/pod-product-compliance
Lightning Source LLC
Chambersburg PA
CBHW020037120526
44589CB00032B/576